MW00813772

Words Of Faith in Wood

by Jeff Paxton

Fox Chapel Publishing Co. Inc.

1970 Broad Street • East Petersburg, PA 17520 • www.foxchapelpublishing.com

© 2004 Fox Chapel Publishing Company, Inc.

Words of Faith in Wood is an original work, first published in 2004 by Fox Chapel Publishing Company, Inc. The patterns contained herein are copyrighted by the author. Artists who purchase this book may make up to three photocopies of these patterns for personal use. The patterns themselves are not to be duplicated for resale or distribution under any circumstances. Any such copying is a violation of copyright law.

Publisher	Alan Giagnocavo
Book Editor	Ayleen Stellhorn
Editorial Assistant	Gretchen Bacon
Cover Design	Jon Deck
Layout	Tucker Yeaworth, Joy Tree Designs

ISBN   1-56523-228-3

Library of Congress Control Number 2003116145

To order your copy of this book,
please send check or money order
for the cover price plus $3.50 shipping to:
Fox Chapel Publishing Company, Inc.
Book Orders
1970 Broad St.
East Petersburg, PA 17520

Or visit us on the web at **www.foxchapelpublishing.com**

Printed in Korea
10 9 8 7 6 5 4 3 2 1

Because scrolling wood and other materials inherently includes the risk of injury and damage, this book cannot guarantee that creating the projects in this book is safe for everyone. For this reason, this book is sold without warranties or guaranties of any kind, express or implied, and the publisher and author disclaim any liability for any injuries, losses or damages caused in any way by the content of this book or the reader's use of the tools needed to complete the projects presented here. The publisher and the author urge all artists to thoroughly review each project and to understand the use of all tools before beginning any project.

Table of Contents

About the Author

Dr. Jeff Paxton lives in Russellville, Arkansas, where he serves as the Senior Pastor of the First Baptist Church of Dover. He has been in full-time ministry for nearly twenty years and has served at his current church for over fifteen years. Dr. Paxton received his Bachelor of Arts Degree in Communication from the University of Memphis, his Master of Divinity Degree from Mid-America Baptist Theological Seminary in Memphis, Tennessee, and his Doctor of Ministry Degree from Luther Rice Seminary in Atlanta, Georgia. He has participated in mission trips in the United States and in countries around the world including India and Guatemala.

In his time away from church work, Jeff enjoys spending time with his wife, Marci, and their two children, Austin and Ashley. He also operates Paxton's Portraits and Projects, a small business from his home that primarily consists of Christian scrollwork and personal portraits cut in wood. He also sells his scrollwork in two booths at a local Collector's Gallery Craft Mall and, as time permits, works several craft shows throughout the year. This is his first book for Fox Chapel Publishing Company.

Readers can contact Jeff at jpaxton@cswnet.com or fbcdover@cswnet.com.

Introduction

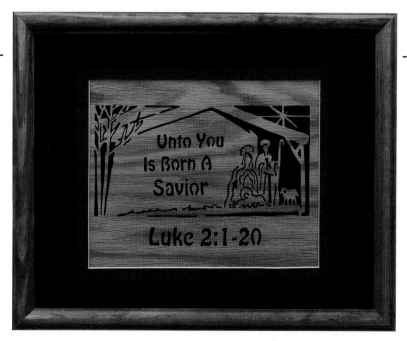

Pattern on page 27

My wife asked me several years ago what I wanted for Christmas. There was nothing that I really needed, but I knew that answer would not satisfy her. I am always working on some project, so she knew that there must be a new tool I had my eye on. Of course, she was right. I had been thinking about a scroll saw for a few months. Scrolling seemed like something I could get into, because I really enjoy working with my hands. I realized that I was by no means a carpenter, but in my mind I thought a scroll saw would not really require a full woodworking shop and common sense told me it would inspire creativity. So I did some research on the Internet, read a few books, and made the decision of which saw I wanted, and under my tree that Christmas morning was one of the most enjoyable gifts my wife has ever given me. That scroll saw was the beginning of my journey into the wonderful world of scroll sawing. My initial thoughts on scrolling turned out to be correct: It doesn't demand a huge workshop, and it certainly does inspire me to be creative. The beauty of scrolling is that there are projects for every skill level. Let me say that this book is not a training man-

ual or a handbook on the scroll saw. There are many books that already cover those areas by individuals who are much more qualified than I. This book takes scrolling in a direction that is near to my heart. I am a pastor and have been in full-time ministry for nearly twenty years. After doing several craft shows through the years and maintaining a couple of booths at a local craft mall, I noticed that my best selling scroll-sawed pieces were ones that had a spiritual message. People were continually asking if I could create a certain type of piece with a specific message. That is when I began to develop my own Christian scroll saw patterns.

One of the things that I noticed about the demand for my work was that people wanted pieces that incorporated Scripture. That was certainly a blessing to me because that was my desire. So people's demands and my desires intersected, and the result is the book you have in your hands. This, too, is what I believe makes this book unique. While there are many wonderful inspirational scroll saw books on the market today, this one is devoted totally to the Scriptures. I have found in my ministry and my scroll sawing that

Pattern on page 28

people at times need to be comforted or encouraged, challenged or inspired. Not only is this what I believe these patterns will do, this has also been the testimony of many who already have these patterns hanging in their homes.

Let me say a final word about the design of the patterns in this book. The patterns I create are specifically designed to be matted and framed. That is the focus of the first project and the 30 ready-to-cut patterns in this book. You can expand the use of these patterns to include other practical projects. I have included instructions for a Bible box and ideas for other ways to use these patterns. Be creative and you can make beautiful plaques or pieces for a shelf, bookcase or desk. While I have found that matted and framed scroll saw pieces sell best at the craft shows in my area, you may wish to make other projects as special gifts for family and friends or as special sale items for your local craft shows. However you decide to finish these patterns, may they be a blessing to you and, in turn, a blessing to others.

Pattern on page 49

Pattern on page 55

Pattern on page 53

Pattern on page 25

Pattern on page 36

Pattern on page 22

Pattern on page 20

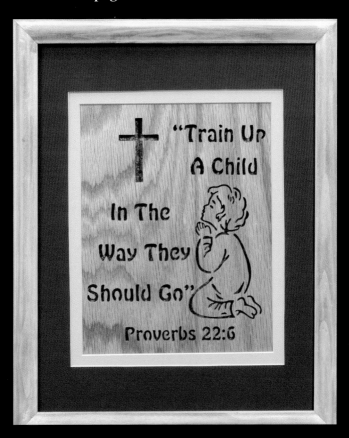

Pattern on page 21

Photo Gallery

Pattern on page 26

Pattern on page 23

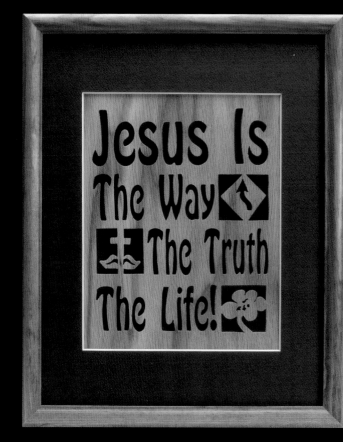

Pattern on page 19

PROJECT ONE: Matted and Framed Pieces

People comment to me on a regular basis that these matted and framed pieces are real "conversation pieces." While that is a blessing to me, I fully understand that it is the message that makes the difference. There are plenty of beautiful things we can put in our homes, but these patterns speak! They proclaim powerful messages; not mine, but those straight from Scripture. Some encourage, others challenge, and many bring comfort to our hearts and homes. My prayer is that these patterns will be a blessing to you as you cut them and also to those who ultimately receive them.

WOOD CHOICE

Most scrollers have their own preference when choosing the wood they want to use for any given project. I have used a variety of woods for projects over the years: some I liked, and some I didn't. Trial and error teaches us much about selecting wood for a successful project, and soon personal preference takes over.

For the matted and framed projects, I use ¼" oak plywood. I have found that there are three benefits to using this type of wood. First, when projects are matted and framed the only real part of the wood a person will see is the beautiful color and grain of the oak surface, not the plywood filler material that shows on the side. Second, projects that are set apart from the frame with a contrasting matte look great when the color of the wood matches the color of the frame. Using oak plywood for the project makes this process easy and gives you an elegant-looking finished piece. And third, the likelihood of oak plywood warping is minimal as opposed to solid oak.

Two other benefits are financial ones. First of all, in the work I do for craft malls and craft shows, I need several pieces of each design. I have found oak plywood to be an excellent wood for stack cutting. Stack cutting allows me to easily cut three pieces at one time, and this saves me valuable time and, as a result, money. Second, instead of purchasing small squares of wood through the mail, I can go to my local lumber store or home center and purchase a 4' x 8' sheet of oak plywood that I get to inspect before I purchase it.

Experience has taught me that there are a couple things to keep in mind when purchasing plywood. Obviously, you'll want to look for a sheet of plywood that is not scuffed up, scratched or defective in any way. Also look for a grain that has a "character" that will be noticeable in the finished project. Finally, shop at a lumberyard or home center that will cut your plywood for you. Most of these types of stores will cut a sheet of plywood two times without charge. I've found it best to ask them to cut a 96"-wide sheet into thirds, resulting in three pieces that are 32" wide each. Make sure that you instruct the salesperson cutting the wood to go very, very slow in order to minimize splintering. Once I'm home, I cut the strips into 45 pieces of wood approximately 9 1/2" x 10 5/8" so that they can be matted and placed comfortably in an 11" x 14" frame.

STACK CUTTING

As I mentioned earlier, oak plywood is great for stack cutting. I have found that cutting three 1/4" pieces of wood at one time works best. To stack cut a pattern, follow the instructions below.

1. Choose three pieces of 1/4" oak plywood.
2. Use 150- or 200-grit sandpaper to smooth out any rough spots.

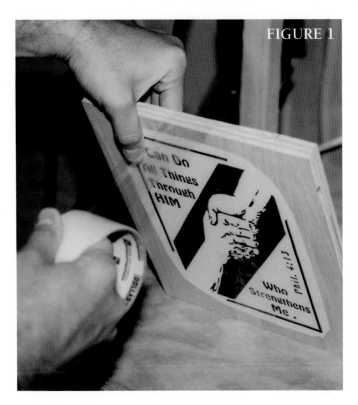

FIGURE 1

3. Position the pattern on each piece of wood to ensure that the grain direction works well with the pattern. The grain should run horizontally with horizontal patterns and vertically with vertical patterns. Turn the wood 180 degrees if necessary to get a better grain pattern.
4. Center the pattern on one piece of wood and glue it in place with an adhesive spray. Avoid poor quality spray glues as the pattern may lift off the wood as you are scrolling.
5. Stack the three pieces of wood, placing the piece with the pattern on top. Be sure the bottoms of the pieces are even. The other three sides do not need to be even.
6. Secure the three pieces of wood by wrapping clear packing tape lengthwise and widthwise across the pieces. (**See Figure 1.**) Press out any air bubbles to prevent dust from gathering and obscuring the lines while you are sawing.
7. Drill starter holes in the waste areas of the pattern. Use a drill press to ensure that your starter holes are drilled perfectly straight through all three pieces of wood. (**See Figure 2.**) A 1/16" or 1/8" drill bit makes a hole through which a plain end scroll saw blade can easily be inserted. In smaller areas, use a #64 drill bit.
8. Make sure your table is level and square to the blade before you begin cutting.

TO MAKE THE PIECES SHOWN IN THIS SECTION, USE THESE PATTERNS:

Lion and Lamb
Pages 29 and 30

Fruit of the Spirit
Pages 31 and 32

Thou Wilt Keep
Page 48

I Will Never Leave You
(I Can Do All Things)
Page 35

BLADE SELECTION

There are many helpful scroll saw handbooks on the market today that extensively discuss the various kinds of blades made for the scroll saw and their appropriate function. The success of a project can very much depend on the proper blade selection, because different blades are designed for different applications.

In my work, I prefer Olson reverse skip tooth blades, #2/0 R and #2R. I have experimented with a variety of blades, and for me, these blades are very easy to control. They hold their line extremely well and make crisp, sharp turns, even when stack cutting. The reverse teeth on these blades minimize splintering, thereby reducing sanding time when the cuts are complete. The only drawback I have found is that the plywood can dull these blades quickly and the blade may have to be replaced before the pattern is completely cut.

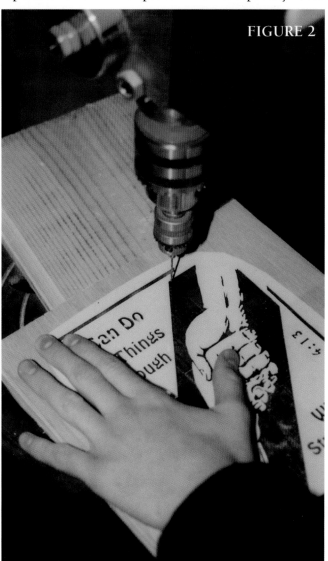

FIGURE 2

There are certainly more aggressive blades on the market, and you'll want to experiment to find out which blade works best for you.

A helpful tip that I have learned concerning blades is to quickly sand the ends to keep them from slipping from the clamp while cutting a project. Take a small piece of 100-grit sandpaper and fold it with the grit to the inside. Then place the end of the blade inside the folded sandpaper. Squeeze your fingers together and pull the blade out, keeping pressure on your fingertips. This motion helps to remove any oil that may have built up on the blade and roughens the surface where the clamp will tighten onto the blade. Do this a couple of times on both ends of the blade, and blade slippage will not be a problem.

THREE CUTTING RULES

The first rule, and one that I always follow, is one that I learned the hard way. Before cutting a project, observe the details of the pattern, note the cuts that seem to be more difficult, and start by cutting these first. There is nothing worse than working many hours on a project only to have it totally ruined if you make a wrong cut on a difficult area that you saved for last.

The most common rule of fretwork—start toward the middle of the pattern and work your way outward—is the second rule to follow. By working your way to the outside cuts from the inside, you ensure that the strength of the wood will not be compromised.

Finally, make the largest cuts your last cuts. Obviously, when a large piece of wood is cut out, it can render the remaining wood of the project very fragile.

FINISHING TIPS

Once the project is completely cut out, it is time to prepare the wood for the finishing touches.

1. Remove the packing tape from the bottom two pieces of wood by melting the adhesive with a hot air gun.

FIGURE 3

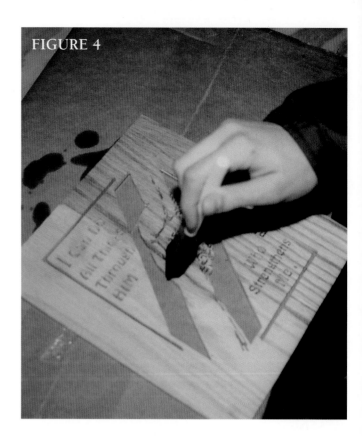

FIGURE 4

2. Remove the pattern and the packing tape from the top piece of wood with a hot air gun or mineral spirits. Remember, some pieces are fragile, so be careful when removing the pattern. (**See Figure 3.**)

3. Remove any residual glue with mineral spirits. (**See Figure 4.**)

4. Sand away any splinters with a folded piece of sandpaper or sandpaper wrapped around a pencil or drill bit.

5. Blow any dust from the piece with an air compressor. Make sure to remove all the dust particles and debris from any small frets or narrow openings.

6. Finally, apply a stain or finish coat of your choice according to the manufacturer's directions. For most of the projects I sell, I simply use a good quality, clear finish spray applied directly to the wood. I usually apply three thin coats. The first coat seals the wood grain and provides a base for the final two coats. This process provides a rich, natural finish that preserves the beauty of the oak grain.

If you choose to use a stain, apply it prior to the spray finish and use only two coats of spray finish. Be creative and try a variety of stains. I have used some of the colored stains with good success. Colored wood accented by a beautifully colored mat adds another dimension to many of these framed scroll saw projects.

MATTING AND FRAMING

For the most part, the patterns in this book are designed to be placed behind an 11" x 14" mat. If photocopied at one hundred percent, these patterns will fit nicely in a regular eleven by fourteen inch mat with the standard opening of 7¹/₂" x 9¹/₂". They certainly can be enlarged and placed behind larger mats in larger frames. Most of the patterns can even be put in an 8" x 10" frame without a mat if they are slightly reduced.

1. Prepare a backing from a piece of felt glued to some cardboard or use a colored mat. Make sure the felt matches or complements the color of the mat border you intend to use.

2. Choose a mat for the piece. Be creative. Select contrasting or complementary colors. I have even splattered paint onto mats and their backings to complement the wood piece. Primary colors are

FIGURE 5

FIGURE 6

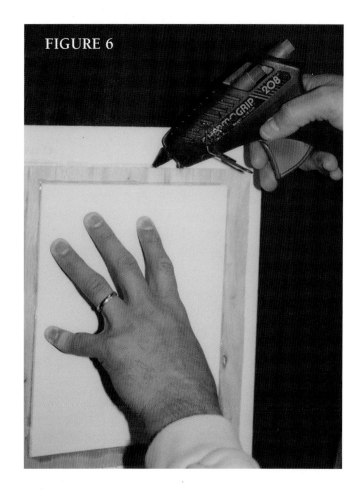

great for children's pieces; red, white and blue are good choices for patriotic pieces.

3. Attach the felt background or mat to the back of the wood design with a glue gun. Make sure that all the cut outs are covered, but that the background piece does not hang over the edge of the wood.

4. If you are matting and framing a word art pattern, glue the wood directly to the colored background. (**See Figure 5.**)

5. Align and center the scrolled piece within the mat opening, then attach the mat border to the wood with a glue gun. Go all the way around the wood with the glue, leaving no gaps so that there will be no openings or cracks when the piece is turned over. (**See Figure 6.**)

6. Clean the glass of the frame, inspect the piece one more time to make sure there are no dust particles on the piece, then place the piece into your chosen frame.

7. Add a hanger made from two small screws and some twenty-gauge wire.

8. Sign the back of your work.

PROJECT TWO: Making a Bible Box

Cutting a box on the scroll saw is now an easy thing to do thanks to the innovative scrolling techniques of Diana Thompson. For this project, I provided a word art pattern of the phrase "Our God Reigns." Diana made the accompanying box from light-colored wood. The words were cut from a dark wood.

CUTTING THE WORDS

Apply the pattern to a piece of ¹⁄₈" wood of your choice with repositionable spray adhesive. Be sure to take advantage of any striping or figure in the grain of the wood. Avoid any splits, cracks, knots or other flaws in the wood.

Before beginning to cut, check that the saw table is square to the blade. You can do this easily and quickly with any tool that has a right angle.

This step is important, especially when the edges of the artwork are raised above the finished surface as they will be for this box. Angled sides resulting from an improperly installed blade will ruin the sharp edges of the pattern.

Cut the inside frets first. Drill starter holes with an appropriately sized drill bit. Carefully cut the frets with a #3R scroll saw blade. As you finish cutting a fret, the pieces will pop out and away from the cut.

When all of the inside frets are cut, move to the outside cut. Try to cut this outline smoothly and in one pass. If you need to stop, break away from the outline before stopping the saw. To restart, carefully cut back into the outline. This will eliminate a rough spot along the outline, a common occurrence if you stop the saw in the middle of a cut.

CUTTING THE BOX

To make a box, the sides are cut first. Apply the pattern on page 15 to 3/4" stock. If you want a deeper box, use wood that is up to 1¼" thick. Use a #5 or a #7 blade, depending on the thickness of the stock you have chosen.

First cut the inside line of the pattern. Do not remove the pattern! Next glue the cut piece of wood to a flat piece of ¼" stock. This second piece of wood will form the bottom of the box. Clamp these pieces and allow them to dry. Now cut the outside line of the pattern. Take note that you are cutting through two layers of wood. This last cut will shape the outside of the box and trim the bottom at the same time.

The lid is cut next. Apply the pattern on page 16 to a piece of ¼" wood. Use a #5R blade for the cuts that make the lid.

First cut the inside line only. Again, do not remove the pattern! Next glue the cut piece of wood to a flat piece of ¼" stock. This second piece of wood will form the top of the box lid. Clamp these pieces and allow them to dry. Now cut the outside line of the pattern. You are cutting through both layers of wood at this point. When you are finished, you will have a lid with a lip that fits perfectly around the outside of the box.

FINISHING TOUCHES

Before finishing the box, consider rounding over the bottom edge of the box and the top edge of the lid. These cuts are a small touch, but they lend to the professional finished look of a nicely made box.

Glue the word art to the top of the box; then, spray the finished box with a clear sealer. Once you have the basic box-making steps mastered, try some of these other ideas.

- Cut a relief-cut image or word in the lid of the box.
- Inlay an image in the lid of the box.
- Change the basic shape of the box to mimic a heart, a cross or another shape.
- Use the alphabets in the back of this book to personalize the box.
- Paint, decoupage or otherwise decorate the box.

1/8" to 1/4" stock for lettering
#3R blade
I used 1/8"

© Jeff Paxton

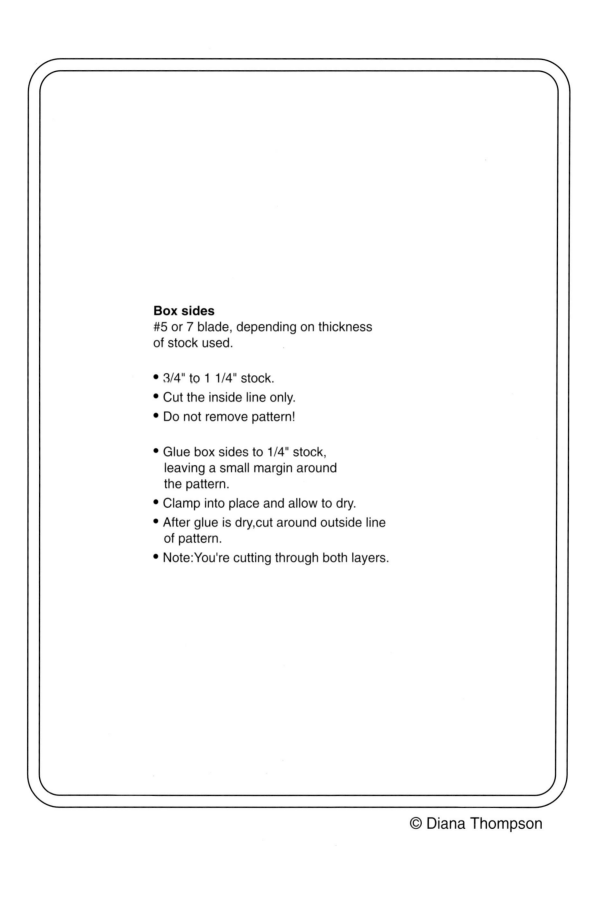

Box sides
#5 or 7 blade, depending on thickness
of stock used.

- 3/4" to 1 1/4" stock.
- Cut the inside line only.
- Do not remove pattern!

- Glue box sides to 1/4" stock,
  leaving a small margin around
  the pattern.
- Clamp into place and allow to dry.
- After glue is dry,cut around outside line
  of pattern.
- Note:You're cutting through both layers.

© Diana Thompson

Lid underside
#5R blade

1/4" stock
- Apply pattern to stock and cut the inside
  line only!
- Do not remove pattern.
- Glue lid underside to another piece of 1/4" stock,
  leaving a small margin around
  the pattern.
- Clamp into place and allow to dry.
- After glue is dry, cut around outside line of pattern.
- Note: You're cutting through both thicknesses.

- Round over upper and lower edges of lid
  and lower box edge with sandpaper to relieve
  the sharp edges. They can also be rounded over
  with a 1/8" round over bit fitted into a rotary tool and
  router table.....which is what I have done here.

© Diana Thompson

ILLUSTRATED SCRIPTURE PATTERNS

As they are presented here, each of the patterns in this section is perfectly sized to fit an 11" x 14" mat with a standard 7½" x 9½" opening, which can then be placed nicely in an 11" x 14" frame. Follow the instructions on pages 7 – 11 if that is your plan.

With little to no modification, you can use these patterns to design and create a number of other projects. Try isolating just an illustration; then, do one of the following.

- Make a card from heavy paper stock.
- Cut an emblem into a notepad.
- Create a luminary or night light.
- Add letters from the alphabets at the back of the book to personalize your work.

"Pray For Your Leaders & Those In Authority"

1 Timothy 2:1-2

© Jeff Paxton

Jesus Is The Way The Truth The Life!

© Jeff Paxton

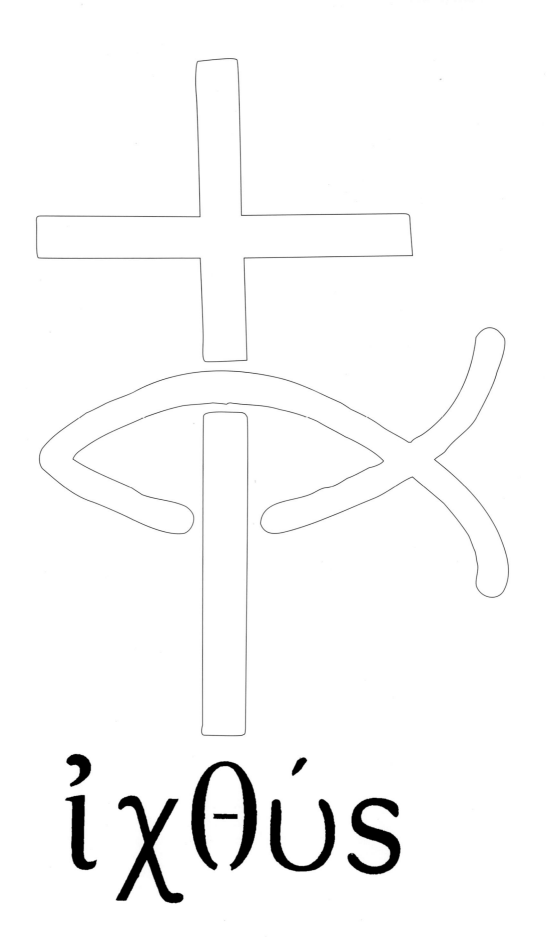

ἰχθύς

© Jeff Paxton

"Train Up A Child

In The Way They Should Go"

Proverbs 22:6

© Jeff Paxton

Behold
I
Come Quickly
Rev. 22:12

© Jeff Paxton

I Have Hidden In My **HEART** **Your Word** That I Might Not Sin Against You

Psalm 119:11

© Jeff Paxton

He Gave Himself
A Ransom For
All 1 Tim 2:6

© Jeff Paxton

Keith & Jackie

"The Two Shall Become One"

May 4, 2002

© Jeff Paxton

© Jeff Paxton

Unto You
Is Born A
Savior

Luke 2:1-20

© Jeff Paxton

Noah's Ark

"They Went In Two By Two"

Genesis 6:2

© Jeff Paxton

The Lion Will

The Lay With

Lamb   Isaiah 11:6

© Jeff Paxton

© Jeff Paxton

The Fruit of the Spirit is Love, Joy, Peace, Patience, Kindness, Goodness, Faithfulness, Gentleness and Self-Control

© Jeff Paxton

© Jeff Paxton

The Lord is my Shepherd

© Jeff Paxton

" I Am The *Light* Of The World "

John 8:12

© Jeff Paxton

I will Never Leave You

Nor Forsake You

Heb. 13:5

© Jeff Paxton

John 8:12

"I am The Light
of the World"

© Jeff Paxton

"King of Kings &
Lord of Lords"
I Tim. 6:15

© Jeff Paxton

Do To Others
as you would have them
Do To You.

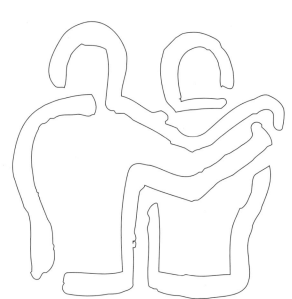

Luke 6:31

© Jeff Paxton

"I Will Lift Up My Eyes To The Hills From Whence Cometh My Strength" Psalm 121:1

© Jeff Paxton

The Prayer of Jabez
(I Chron. 4:10)

"Lord, Bless Me Indeed,
Enlarge My Territory, Be
With Me, Keep Me
From Evil That I May
Cause No Pain, And
God Granted His Request."

© Jeff Paxton

I was glad when they said unto me "Let us go into the house of the Lord."

Psalm 122:1

© Jeff Paxton

"Behold, Children Are A Gift From The Lord"

Psalm 127:3

© Jeff Paxton

"Train Up A Child

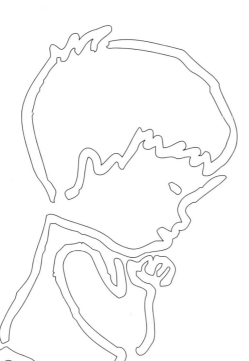 In The Way He Should Go"

Proverbs 22:6

© Jeff Paxton

"I Bring You Good News of Great Joy"
Luke 2:10

© Jeff Paxton

"For Unto You Is Born A Savior Who Is Christ The Lord"

Luke 2:11

© Jeff Paxton

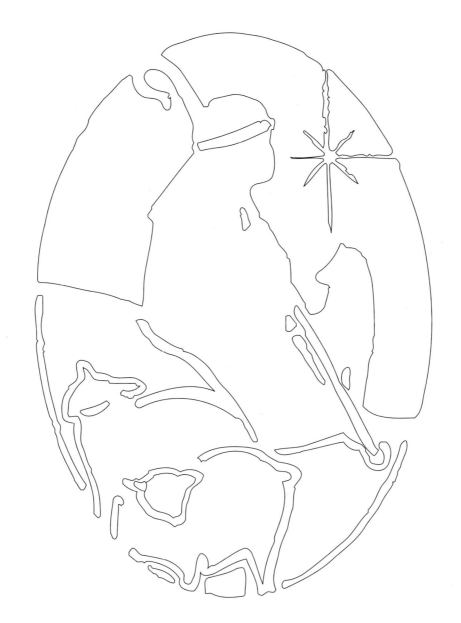

"We Have Seen His Star"

Matt. 2:2

© Jeff Paxton

WORD ART SCRIPTURE PATTERNS

As with the illustrated Scripture patterns in the previous section, each of the patterns in this section are perfectly sized to fit within an 11" x 14" mat with a standard 7$1/2$" x 9$1/2$" opening, which can then be placed nicely in an 11" x 14" frame. The instructions on pages 7 – 11 will tell you how to create framed and matted pieces.

For something different, try one of the following ideas.

- Mount the words on a scrolled or store-bought box.
- Make a desk plaque from dark or highly figured wood.
- Design a wooden album or scrapbook cover.
- Cut a door sign for a friend or relative.
- Use the patterns in the back of the book to scroll your favorite Scripture.

© Jeff Paxton

© Jeff Paxton

© Jeff Paxton

© Jeff Paxton

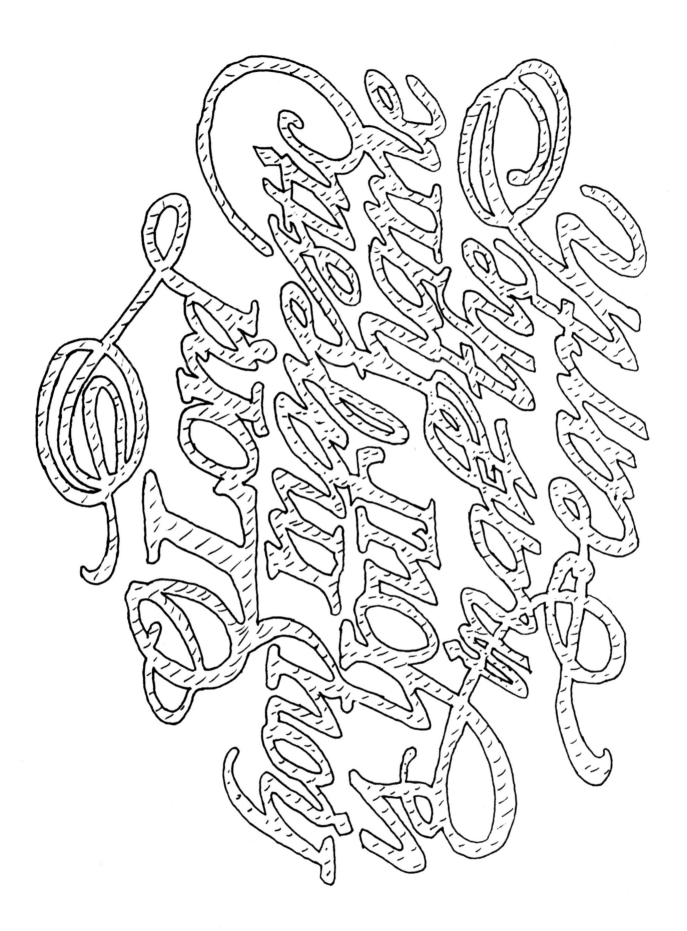

© Jeff Paxton

Lord Teach us to Pray

© Jeff Paxton

© Jeff Paxton

Bless The Lord O My Soul & All That Is Within Me.

Psalm 103:1

© Jeff Paxton

As for Me And My House We Will Serve the Lord. Josh. 14:6

© Jeff Paxton

O COME
let us WORSHIP
& BOW down,
let us KNEEL
before the LORD
OUR
MAKER
Psalm 95:6

© Jeff Paxton

"O Lord, Our Lord, How Majestic Is Your Name In All The Earth"
Psalm 8:1

"Call To Me And I Will Answer You, And I Will Show You Great And Mighty Things.

Jeremiah 33:3

© Jeff Paxton

"Be Strong and Courageous! Do Not Tremble Or Be Dismayed, For the Lord Your God Is With You Wherever You Go." Joshua 1:9

© Jeff Paxton

Words of Faith in Wood

A B C D E

F G H I J

K L M N

O P Q R S

T U V W X

Y Z

a b c d e f g h i

j k l m n o p q

r s t u v w x y z

1 2 3 4 5 6 7 8

9 0 :

A B C D E

F G H I J K

L M N O P

Q R S T U

V W X Y Z

a b c d e f
g h i j k l
m n o p q
r s t u v w
x y z

Scroll Saw Ready Numbers

1 2 3 4 5
6 7 8 9 0 :

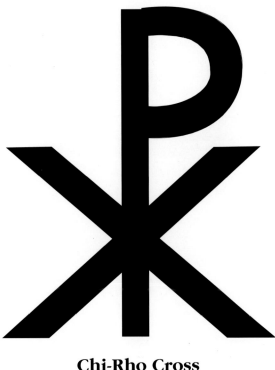

Chi-Rho Cross

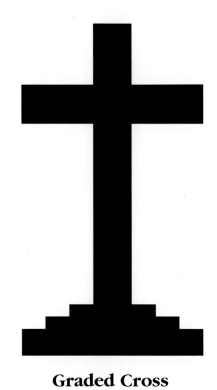

Graded Cross

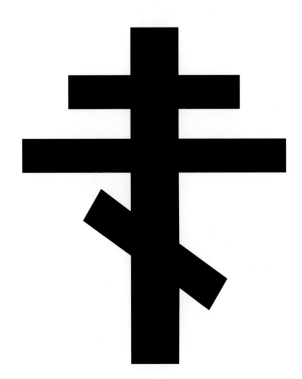

Orthodox Cross

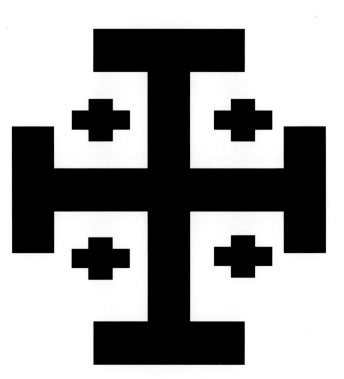

Jerusalem Cross

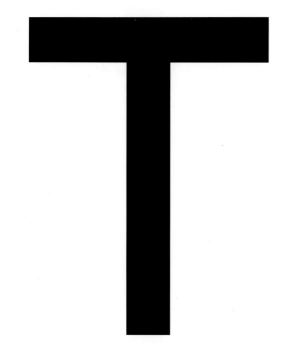

St. Anthony's Cross

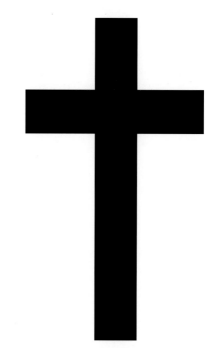

Latin Cross

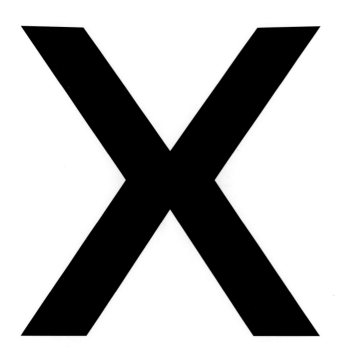

St. Andrew's Cross

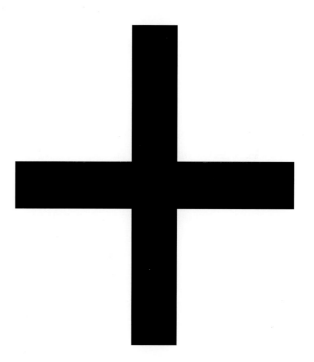

Greek Cross

More Great Project Books from Fox Chapel Publishing

- **Intarsia Workbook by Judy Gale Roberts:** Learn the art of intarsia from the #1 expert, Judy Gale Roberts! You'll be amazed at the beautiful pictures you can create when you learn to combine different colors and textures of wood to make raised 3-D images. It features 7 projects and expert instructions. Great for beginners!
ISBN: 1-56523-226-7, 72 pages, soft cover, $14.95.

- **Scroll Saw Portraits by Gary Browning:** Learn how to use a computer or photocopier to change any photograph into a pattern for your scroll saw. Includes pattern-making techniques, tips on which photos make good patterns, and 55 portrait patterns.
ISBN: 1-56523-147-3, 96 pages, soft cover, $14.95.

- **Seashore and Nautical Patterns for the Scroll Saw by William Hofferth:** Over 50 seaside beach patterns for the scroll saw including lighthouses, seashells, boats, shore-birds, nautical symbols, shipwrecks, divers, fishermen, lifeguards, and many others. Great ideas for practical and decorative items such as an antique lobster trade sign, a ship's wheel welcome sign, and more.
ISBN: 1-56523-190-2, 72 pages, soft cover, $12.95.

- **300 Christian & Inspirational Patterns by Tom Zeig:** Create inspiring works of art on your scroll saw with this book which includes more than 300 never before-published designs, a history of Christian symbols, and a glossary of religious symbols and colors.
ISBN: 1-56523-063-9, 173 Pages, soft cover, $14.95

- **Scroll Saw Holiday Puzzles by Tony and June Burns:** You'll be scrolling throughout the year with this festive collection of scroll saw puzzles for the holidays! From New Year's Eve and Christmas to Valentine's Day, Easter, and Halloween, you'll find over 25 delightful puzzle patterns for over 15 holidays and seasons. Basic scrolling information such as choosing a blade, safety and tips also included!
ISBN: 1-56523-204-6, 72 pages, soft cover, $14.95.

- **Custom Wooden Boxes for the Scroll Saw by Diana Thompson:** Classical and whimsical boxes fill the pages of this new book by author and scroll saw artist Diana Thompson. Step-by-step directions show you how to create these boxes using just a scroll saw; additional directions address using common woodshop equipment, such as band saws and a router. A special section on wood introduces you to the colors, grains, and characteristics of common and exotic woods.
ISBN: 1-56523-212-7, 72 pages, soft cover, $17.95.

- **Scroll Saw Workbook 2nd Edition by John A. Nelson:** The ultimate beginner's scrolling guide! Hone your scroll saw skills to perfection with the 25 skill-building chapters and projects included in this book. Techniques and patterns for wood and non-wood projects!
ISBN: 1-56523-207-0, 88 pages, soft cover, $14.95.

- **Country Mosaics for Scrollers and Crafters by Frank Droege:** Bless your friends, neighbors and even your own home with these wooden plaques symbolizing faith, love, and prosperity! Over 30 patterns for hex signs, marriage blessings, house blessings and more included.
ISBN: 1-56523-179-1, 72 pages, soft cover, $12.95.

- **Inspirational Scroll Saw Projects by John A. Nelson:** These expressions of faith and hope will be treasured for generations. Included with this book are over 40 projects including ready-to-use patterns, detailed instructions, and band saw patterns for classic Christian symbols.
ISBN: 1-56523-112-0, 58 pages, soft cover, $9.95

- **A Woodworker's Guide to Making Traditional Mirrors and Picture Frames by John A. Nelson:** A sourcebook of patterns for woodworkers that features plans for mirrors and frames. Learn the basics behind cutting wood for mirrors and frames, and then use the included measured drawings to create your own.
ISBN: 1-56523-223-2, 112 pages, soft cover, $17.95.

CHECK WITH YOUR LOCAL WOODWORKING STORE OR BOOK RETAILER
Or call 800-457-9112 • Visit www.foxchapelpublishing.com